Scattered Ink

Poetic Works of Kindred

Table of Contents

i.   Unreleased Bonus Material

ii.   Nature

iii. Dark Matters

iv. Inspire

v.   Irregularities

vi. Love

For my family, and all who have inspired me to be better.

Unreleased Poems and Quotes

Know Fear

When the pillars give way
and the darkness falls in
fear can never hold sway
on your fire within.

Oxygen

My feather-tip touch,
light as oxygen on your hips.
Your heat-laden breath
falls encumbered from your lips.

Reflections

Is she truly mine own
or does she belong
instead
to a more formidable
version of myself -
a lingering reflection
of my visage
still twisting 'round
her subconscious?
Has she been betrayed
by her own memory -
a memory of times gone;
a dream of a man gone
and never to return?

Linguist

If I must construct a new language
to make you truly believe,
then that is what I shall do.

Spectrum

I don't feel the blues
the way most souls do.
I feel the entire spectrum
all at once.

Break Apart

Don't ever pull this from my grasp,
I could not handle the damage.
My bones would splinter as they coped
and my skin would shatter like glass.

Don't ever walk away from my life,
I would suffocate under that burden.
My soul would empty into the grisly air
as the world I knew was torn asunder.

Do not leave me lonesome and wounded
in this treacherous place -
the person you helped me become
would surely break apart.

Illuminating

Cool wind moves her hair
The moon shines light on her face
Revealing beauty

Maestro

On the fourth day,
God painted the sky with stars.
Mere practice for a greater achievement -
His masterpiece simply titled

You.

Each day you are born anew.
Let go of your past.
Through faith, you are free.

It matters not
when you begin
so long as you
never give in.

I will reap the light I have sewn,
someday before the Lord.

Fullness preys not
on the meek of heart.
So love, laugh, give and be full.

What do you have
if not love in your heart?
What do you give
if not all from the start?

Nature

The Ruler of All Kings

"This way." it says,
the wind to the storm.
"You are not but swells
of anger beating on the shore.
Come with me and spill your
wrath with precision."
"I need you not." it bellows,
the storm to the wind.
What are you that means
to push with might you can't
claim as your own?
I am the strength that
pounds clean the very
atmosphere."
And the thunder clapped.
And the wind howled.
"Follow me!" it demands,
the wind of the storm.
I am the catalyst behind
all that is life. Dare not to
challenge a force such as I.
The earth is mine to spin."
"Bother me not." it says,
the storm to the wind.
With capricious havoc
I hammer the land;
The earth is my canvas
and I paint the ruin."
And the wind crushed.
And the lightning smite.
"Enough." it commands,
the earth to the storm.
"Silence." it says,
the earth to the wind.
"I am supreme
where the wind meets the land.
I am the law
where the storm spills its life.
I am alpha
where all things begin
and I am omega

where it all will soon end."
And the earth rose up,
its fury bled unto the ignorant.
Anguish swept over all
that could witness.
And the wind wept.
And the storm stopped.

Plight of the Roofless

You seem abnormal,
slightly off-kilter.
You frantically pace the grass
unable to keep your own speed.
You are dirty,
possibly never showering
in your entire life.
You find food virtually anywhere;
on the ground, in a dumpster,
in a tree, if need be.
Amid countless twitches and face scratches,
you shove it into your mouth
without a care who may be watching.
If you were a human,
you would be ignored,
maybe even ridiculed.
But you're a squirrel,
so we think you're cute.

A Season Passing

What is this?
A delicate chipmunk
rustling in the parched leaves,
mouth stuffed with the feast of fall.
Do you see how he prances,
see how he dances
to the tune of a
season passing?

And there, atop
the mighty hemlock
that grows naked as the year goes by,
pounds a redheaded woodpecker
hammering bark.
Do you see the chips fly
from the meticulous effort
as he prepares his home for the
season passing?

From a distant pit of flames,
somewhere down the dirt-laden path,
travels the incense created by the scorching
of crippled leaves once green with life.
Can you smell the dry, sweet aroma
of maple and oak and of sycamore as it
floats with the smoky remains of a
season passing?

I can feel the times changing
with each gust that crimps my shirt.
I can sense the natural order of life
in everything that I witness
and can feel the beautiful disorder
of everything I cannot control.
Life is as precious and as wonderful as a
season passing.
As wonderful as a
season passing.

And Nature Too

Many pictures of winter things
in my head where mountains sing;
in my head where birches bend,
covered in snow, the winter's sting.

So many snowflakes fall from the sky
in the woods that a child plays by.
So many snowflakes cover his hair -
so many snowflakes that soon will die.

Insectual Being

An insect curls in the throes of death.
A life brought before its final breath.
A cycle extinguishes what is left.

The creature twitches its legs.
A mother fears for her eggs.
Her spirit silently begs.

Nature takes its course
no matter the will
or immovable force,
emptying essence
no matter the source.

But there is grace in the dying
behind a woeful cry;
a rebirth, though underlying,
before its final sigh.

So This is October

I've never known what virtue
hides in a season
or how self forgiveness
waits beyond long silence.
Neither are things I've
ever grasped
nor cared enough to try.
But now, I break the leaves under
my feet and smile at the sound.
A sound I have not truly
appreciated for so long.

I embrace the approaching
bitterness of the chill.
It reminds me of my past;
lessons I should never forget;
memories that travel the breeze.

The wind feels empty where I am,
but I no longer hold its hand.
It shall have to sell pain somewhere else
for I have consumed all that I can take.
I will not wait to breathe it in,
but I will become full again.

So they tell me this is October -
the death of leaves all around me,
the cold assailing my lungs.
It feels different than I remember.
Even the smell of it has changed
with my loneliness.
But I will strive to find
the beauty
in even the smallest
of hollowed acorns.

While Wandering I Happen Upon Myself

The rain has been ferocious
on this crisp June day.
Falling with intent
not just to saturate,
but to sting.
But I like the coolness
on my back.
My feet have grown their own brain,
wanting to walk in this wetness.
I oblige their calm
yearnings.

The road following the creek,
which is busting at the seams,
is lined with weeds
and goldenrods
and trappers with enormous
overgrown petals
sheltering their patch of earth
from dampness.
My feet carry me through trails
lining the bustling stream;
trails I have ignored for too long.
Acorn shells and dead leaves
not yet drown by the rain
crack and bust under my weight.
I adore the sound.

I come upon a tree
deep in the woods.
Fog from nearby rapids
wants to choke the trunk
of this gentle beast.
It is old and strong
and wise to everything
that has passed its branches.
Someone once tore the bark
in an oval dinner plate fashion.
The wide scar left
by lovers long ago
still marks the underbelly.

They had such foolish dreams
that they carved them
into nature's hide.

Walking on, I come upon
a clearing where the rain
slows its banter
and the sun breaks through
the grayness of memory.
There, I see a boy.
A young teen on the brink of love,
on the edge of loss.
It is remarkable how I've grown,
yet everything remains the same.

Lust by Night, Rich by Day

I would, if I were able,
cease the spinning of the earth.
Shut down the night in all its wonder
to prolong the glorious thunder.
And the rain would freeze amid the air
for all to witness a natural birth
of a beautiful storm poised to break -
a blanket for the stars in nature's wake.

Patiently the sun would wait
with buds to blossom and larks to sing
as I feast upon the awesome glory
that a storm filled night can bring.

But there is also beauty to be found
as the sun bestows light unto the ground
and the once magnificent storm gives way
for the spider to spin her illustrious web.
For me to anticipate what the wind will say
and hear tunes that sprout from a cardinal's neb.
So why not also halt the coming day
when my lust for night does ebb?
Then my absent wealth could spring anew
for each bright day holds riches, too.

Dark Matters

Here Come the Hounds

Trapped inside
forced to hide
fears collide
with silent sounds
pain resounds
here come the
hounds.

A mask of fears
hides the tears
ugly years
show the pain
such disdain
no longer sane.

Shallow breathing air
crying breaking stare
I turn but no one's there.

Howling breaks the night
my pain again in sight
succumb to darkness light.

I hear the silent sounds
in my heart where pain resounds
once again here come the hounds.

Daybreak Without You

Daybreak is finally approaching.
This night has been a long one, indeed.
Sleep was not kind to these weary eyes.
This pillow was dented time and again.

Mournful dreams broke me from slumber,
but the light of day will sprout just the same.
Colors of life will spew forth
giving pleasure to passing viewers.
Though that spectrum will not be as sweet,
not for me.

The sun will peek above the hilltops
and warmth will spread across the land,
but somehow it will not be as warm,
not for me.

Just as every night has been restless for so long,
so too, shall every daybreak be a lonely failure.
I must spend each night and each day alone
for that is what I am without you.
That is what I will be, without you.
That is what I have always been -
without you.

Ominous Omega

Smoke screen air
betrays your senses
as you breathe in deep
the putrid stench of death.
Rubble loosely pops
under your bare feet -
each fiery step
singes them deeper.
The rocky, black-red walls
rise unyieldingly upward.
They tower above
mocking your insignificance.
Searing orange coal-ash
floats with intent.
Each flake of fire dust
burns a hole in your flesh
like a skewer through
freshly poached pork.
It is flesh painted black
from sin.

Each hateful thought.
Every painful word.
All the thoughtless actions.

They have left you marked;
branded with an undying rank.
The beastly ape god,
the Lord of Death,
awaits your organs.
He shall feast endlessly.
For you
there is no ominous omega,
only an ominous eternity.
My God, what have you done?

Sorrow of One

This is a tale of the sorrow of one.
The story of my life absent from her.
I stand alone with a trembling body
waiting for the end to occur.

I miss her like a broken clock misses time.
I feel like an apple without its core.
My reason is clouded without my rhyme.
My knees are embedded in the floor.

I hear her voice across the heartache
and it sounds like mine;
hiding sorrow that could drown an army,
buried deep inside.

Lightning once crashed upon a separate plane,
another dimension within my heart.
She was restless and untamed.
Like electric fire needing but a spark.

Rolling, tumbling, and swirling -
so much life filled these veins.
Now I'm shackled by an unrelenting sorrow
and this sorrow binds with many chains.

Trust the Blackness Within

Numbness squanders my emotion.
I feel nothing but emptiness.
It swirls about the atmosphere
casting a blackness over my crippled mind.

Troubling thoughts ooze from my pores
drowning the world in infinite sorrow.
Trust is the breath that escapes my lungs.
My chest caves from the pain of a new kind.

Learn to trust the blackness within
if you want it to consume you throughout.
Let dishonesty coil around your skull
if you desire the feeling of going blind.

The blackness within will hinder your passion
as it slithers in and out of your heart.
Embrace the blackness within
if it is not love that you wish to find.

A Month Between

A month between
every day, every dream,
every heartache that I've seen.

A season passing,
a fool is asking,
while the devil is laughing.

A day away.
A heart goes astray.
The predator takes the prey.

Twelve months go by.
Each brings grey to the sky,
leaves a broken man asking "why?"

A month between
every day, every dream.
A month between.

The Willows Weep for Me

The willows weep for me.
They howl as you choose to be free.
Their swaying limbs dust the ground,
and in the lonely breeze
they make a somber sound.
An echo of tears as they fall
and crash in a sea of regret.
They drown out my final call
with a chorus I'll never forget.

They ache for the love
that leaves with you
and from the sadness
that burns me through.
Their roots run deep
into my soul,
with your pain,
consuming me whole.

They scream as you drift into the sea,
but the willows only weep for me.

Virginity

Take this virginity of life.
Take it and break it.
Rape it.
Rape it until nothing is left.
Teach me to live as you have.
Teach me to wallow in such
self loathing and insecurity
that I want to burst at the seams
with its sticky venom.
Then show me how to hide it
while I soak up the putrid liquid
of a rotting life like a sponge.
Take this virginity of life
and break it until I learn
how to die the way that you are.

Realization

It's dark in here.
Black as night -
blacker still, as pitch.
It's cold and confined.
The air is stale and stifling.
I can barely breathe.

My chest is tight.
My breaths are shallow.
My heart is racing,
pulse pounding.
Fever building to a cold sweat.
Stubborn lungs
won't compress.
I'm suffocating.
Deafening confusion
quiets my throat
then

panic.

My ankles crack as I kick,
finger nails splinter above me.
Yearning lungs strain
in a dance of rhythmic constraint.

Realization quells hysteria

and peaceful silence
erupts within
my coffin.

Save Me from the Ape

Save me from the ape,
the beastly god of death.
I can no longer wait.
I will have nothing left.

Save me from the wave,
the tide is coming in.
There is no escape,
no way that I can win.

Save me from the ape,
this monster hiding within.
Drain me from your lake,
your shallow pool of sin.

Save me from the ache.
Pull the blade out from my chest.
Release me from your hate.
Put my crumbling soul at rest.

Quiet

One day,
there will be nothing left
for us to rewind to.
As we pause the late night turmoil
you pull the knife from my back
and apologize again.
"Let's go back. I can try harder."
you cry.
I've heard that before.
An eerie echo of ache in my mind
telling me to say,
"No. Not this time.
I can't do this anymore."
Too long I've hurt alone
in my straight jacket of depression.
"Not this time." is what I should say.
But I nod, quietly.
I sob, quietly.
I die, quietly.

The Murder of a Peaceful Heart

Somewhere inside the icy depths
of a chest that's long been stabbed
faintly quivers a heart
with no purpose left to give.
Struggling to go beyond the pain
in search for hope again.
Fighting for the breath
it so desperately needs to live.

Love brought the murder of my peaceful heart
before it ever had the chance to truly beat.
Now silence overthrows my being
and a blindly cherished victory
is seen more clearly as defeat.

Beaten to misery, but not completely broken,
this organ cries out for peace in the night.
Now that this ache has been awoken,
the pen that I hold yields no might.

Butterfly Deceased

The monarch goes in pain,
bound before another train.
Forced where traffic permits -
currents hold an ugly trend.

A young mind lost in the crowd,
a butterfly deceased is the end.
A heart aches, needing a friend -
a butterfly deceased is the end.

I Crawl Upon my Belly

I crawl upon my belly
across the sands of time.
I crawl upon my belly
and see a life as scarred as mine.

I lay upon my back
and let the sand cover my face.
I lay upon my back
and give in to my disgrace.

You crawl upon your belly
and wonder why you cannot stand.
You crawl upon your belly
because you will not take my hand.

Suicide by Night-light

I see them creeping.
Walking and sleeping.
Some of them weeping.

All of them dead,
but all in my head.
I fear that I've said
far too much.

I hear them cry.
Their rivers run dry,
then wither and die.

So far deep inside
I need them to hide.
Forever reside,
never to touch.

The damage is done.
I know that they've won.

Pull out my gun.

When Pain Dims the Light

When pain dims the light
you will see my face no more.
When hope fades at night
I'll be left outside your door.

When pain blurs your sight
and love is all that you see
you will look within yourself,
but you will never see me.

Black

I thought I would glow
at the center of your world.
Instead, I crumbled
to the floor of my demise.
I should have known
the black could not contain me
and that all hope
would be crushed before my eyes.

The clouds were too thick
for us to part.
Your sky was too dark
for me to glide.
Those mountains were steep
that tired my heart.
The hate was too strong
for you to hide.

The black was too cold
for me to bear.
Your life is too dark
to ever see me there.

Death of an Angel

He screamed to the heavens
pointing the blame at something
he did not understand;
an invisible scapegoat.
He shook his finger at the sky
not able to control his fear;
not able to stop his tears.
Each tragedy constructed a wall
around his faith.
He could not remember the meaning
of love or beauty.
They became obscure concepts
after his most recent pain.
Guardian angels did not exist
for him anymore.
All that was God and love
seemed like blind faith -
something he would not accept.
He turned against the only form of
inspiration he had ever known.
He stopped believing
and slowly began to die.
Unexplainable misfortune took away
the only things that he loved.
Misguided anger took away what remained,
including his will to carry on.

One Thousand Nails

One thousand nails
prick my skin.
One thousand pains
sink within.

A journey lost
from such cruel time.
A heavy frost
upon my rhyme.

One thousand nails
on which I sleep.
How much pain
can one man keep?

The answer lies,
but don't we all?
When truth is found
the honest fall.

One thousand flies
surround the blood.
One thousand eyes
observe the flood.

One thousand nails
live in my breath.
One thousand times
I've cheated death.

Perhaps, I am Alone

What is this consuming emptiness
overpowering my being?
It feels so familiar
like a brother -
like a brother stabbing me in the chest.
Perhaps I have failed once again.
Perhaps I am broken
and I must be torn.
Perhaps I should have loved you
more than my heart could know.
Perhaps I should have embraced the fighting
more than my arms would condone.
And the scheduled heartache
that knew just when to spawn -
perhaps I should have loved it, as well.
Perhaps, but what then?
Allow my soul to burn
in the heat of your eyes?
Let my heart be worn
as the armor of your disguise?
Oh, then I would surely become
the pitiful wretch you think I will be.
It would awaken the hate
that I always feared I would see.
I would ask myself endlessly,
"Just what is the cause
of this deafening silence?"
Though the answer will always be
far too easy to find -
A loving sound remains unknown,
so perhaps, I am alone.

Serious Matters

"Don't take it so seriously."
she said, patting her stomach.
I smiled at her gesture
while my skin grew pasty white.
She licked her red lips
and threw an evil smile back.
I asked,
"How could I not take this seriously?
Do you not realize what you have done?"
"Apparently not." I replied,
answering my own question.
"After all, you just ate my heart."

Private Strings

Private strings
spin a fierce melody.
A tune played with richness.

Lustful wings
flap with great memory.
Wind forced through the stillness.

Private strings
ring a song above my lobe,
then cease the wonder to my disdain.

And lustful wings
run out of the will to goad,
letting me free-fall in solitary pain.

Inspire

Hope Reborn, the Beginning

Unwelcome dreams
have made me numb.
I feel that now
the time has come
to let the wind
give flight to wings
attached to scars
from bloody stings.
On my back
the whip took pride
in creating there
a calloused hide.

And so I now,
with God's good will,
seal the wounds
where blood did spill
and take a flight
away from here,
letting go
of all I fear.

And soon, I know
that day will come -
from dreams I'll be
no longer numb.

This is How it Feels

This is how it feels
to love, but not love.
To speak and not be heard.
To propose, but receive no answer.
This is how it feels
to live and die in one existence,
yet still walk the earth.
To have lungs compress, then decompress,
but bring forth no air to pump the blood.
This is how it feels
to have beauty brought within grasp
only to have no hands for its seizure.
To go to bed full of passion
and wake as the dried out core
of what used to be.
This is how it feels
to want what can't be had
and to refuse what should be taken.
To go from the brink of the final option
to stumbling upon a mound of new possibilities.

When the Music Stops

Where do you go when the path ends?
Make your own and push ahead.

What do you need when you have all you want?
You give a little back, instead.

What do you say when you run out of words?
Create a new language, all your own.

Whom do you love when your love is broken?
Learn to love yourself, or remain all alone.

How do you live when you lose something dear?
You live to find it anew, starting within.

What do you do when the music stops?
You put on another album and let it begin.

The Moth

A moth is resting on a wall.
It is furry and brown
and splattered with intricate white designs.
Its eyeballs move without visible motion
spying on me as I spy on it.
I pace in front of the tiny creature,
back and forth.
It does not move.
I can sense it reading me
like a bible verse.
"What do you want?"
it finally asks
without uttering a word.
"I do not know." I reply, stunned.
"Then live until you find the answer."
says the moth resting on a wall.

Dodo Bird

Responsibility hits me quick,
like the prize from a cracker jack box.
It was not expected,
but not shunned to the side.
I'll take it as a gift, as a chance.
I'll see it as a doorway into myself
so I can see what there is
and discover what there could be.
Maybe I'll once again learn something
of who I am and what I am capable of.
Perhaps another piece to the puzzle
of individual mystery will fall
and smash down into place.
Snug and secure,
like the overstuffed dodo bird, too fat to fly.
Frail, tired wings too stressed by the added weight
to carry the burden.
Life is nothing to take lightly.
I heard that somewhere and decided to laugh.
Then I woke up, paralyzed by epiphany,
and laughed again at the irony of it all.
But this new direction is a blessing
wrapped up within my own fears,
my own short-comings.
Even if it doesn't take us to bliss,
it will take us somewhere.
And the lessons learned along the way
will be enough to make me smile,
will be enough to make me live.

Live, and Live Free

Abandoned, desperate, alone -
feelings too often I've known.
How does one live with the pain
or deal with the sorrow?
There is fear inside I cannot contain
and I dread the thought of tomorrow.

My loneliness spreads, thickening.
Her sinful acts are sickening.
My solemn candle is flickering.
To a cliff, the water is trickling;

flowing to the end then is gone,
shot like a helpless fawn,
used like a hapless pawn.

On my face the scars are shown.
In my heart the throes are sewn.
Forbidden fruit has been taken,
and her soul has been forsaken.

I need someone to hear me,
I need my heart to pound.
I want someone to save me,
but the only one I've found
is lost in another's grasp,
she is held in another's clasp.

With this plague inside my chest
the ache is too much to bear.
It cannot heal without rest,
now countless cracks reside there.

My patience is beginning to slip.
These hands are losing their grip.
The threads are ready to rip.

But against all odds
they do not fray.
Those plights of agony
will not hold sway.

And with the breaking dawn
a sound rings on and on -
the truth of what should be,
a voice that begs of me
to finally live, and live free.

Hope Called to Me

Pain called to me,
but I listened not.
"Remember." it begged of me,
then a picture was caught.
A black oil background,
red demons running about.
I shunned it to the side
when hate began to leak out.
For hope had called to me
somewhere in recent time.
I followed it close
and heard its peaceful rhyme.

Hope called to me
and I knew the language it bore.
Words that were hard to understand,
but I grew to so adore.

The pain spoke loudly,
but I resisted that sound.
Hope had already called to me
and by that hope I was bound.

The Moth, Revisited

"Why is this fleeting life
so hard to for you to see?"
the moth inquired,
gazing keenly at me.

"I fear I do not know
what that answer could be."
I replied with hushed tone,
so delicately.

He flapped his brown wings
as I stood by the sea.
Then he spoke with no mouth,
but his words still broke free.

They whispered through my brain
and I must agree -
that my eyes have been closed
oh so selfishly.

Live Again

He is beaten, bruised and battered.
His slim arms are wrinkled and tan -
the visage of a fading man.
His dream of greatness tattered.

Defeat has found where he has been.
It caught him slipping on icy age,
caught him struggling to turn the page.
But he has vowed to live again.

Somewhere in the fear and weakness,
somehow through the empty bleakness
he found the strength to fight the sin.
He found the strength to live again.

Trying always to look within,
he will rise and live again.

Dreams Resurrected

Tomorrow waits
beyond my fear
for me to have
a chance to hear.

Not silent dreams
or broken schemes,
they hurt no more
and no more implore.

For pleaful cries
that break the hollow
attract no flies
where I will wallow.

That place within
my growing soul
where dreams rebuild
and faith is whole.

The World of Unfinished Thoughts (The Last Moth)

He is back.
I can feel his insect eyes
dotting my frame,
watching me, yet not.
The silent flutter of his wings
brushes past my ear
and I know why he has come.
Fragile appendages
and a spotted thorax.
The body of a moth, for sure,
with the brain of God himself.

"Never think such thoughts."
he commanded, absent of sound.
"Such things are not born
of gentile minds and neither
should they reside."

He hears my very thoughts,
so he knows that I am lost.
Silence follows for ten seconds,
then he speaks,

"You feel that you are lost,
yet everyday you walk the same path."

"Yes." I thought,
"I know."

"You walk with your feet
when it is your heart that knows the way."

"I know."

"You think that you are lost,
but there is only one path below you.
No matter how often you falter,
it is still the same path. It is still your way.
There is but one path, you decide
where it leads."

"I know."

"If you know, then why am I here?" the moth inquired.

I thought on this a moment, then he was gone.
The truth was always there
in the world of unfinished thoughts.

Hope Reborn, the Final Words

My hope reborn,
I can't believe
that hell would take
from me its leave
to slink away
into the night,
to follow pain
in human plight.

But it did
with yellow skin,
faded quick
out from within
and I have
been left alive
for truth to seek
and love to strive.

Tomorrow - I
will fear it not
for hell has sold
its final lot.
I'll simply laugh
and to life say,
"There is no use,
my hope will stay."

Irregularities (Misc.)

Fire Within the Ice

There is fire within the ice,
so to your hand only once.
For if I dare touch it twice
I'll be scolded for months.

There is ugliness about such beauty
that chills me to the bone.
Shall I tempt my fate once more?
I would rather be alone.

The Fool Who Dares To Dream

Why does it hurt to breathe
and why must I sleep to have a dream?
Because breathing is a sign of life
and it is this life that makes me scream.

For a dream too great is but an anchor,
it only serves to hold me down.
Better to experience this at rest
so that only I will know the clown.

Goodbye

Goodbye, impossible dream.
Goodbye, impossible love.
Remember me always
as the one who wanted to try;
as the one who would never
claim the prize.

Victory Internal

Northern winds rap on the window
as I speak into the headset.
The room is oblivious to my words.
They only hear their own thoughts,
clouded by their imperfections
of the body and mind
and by how poorly
their day has been going.
This job is much too easy for them.

I tap my foot once and tug on my collar.
It loosens, but not enough to
release the tension that had been boiling.
Those nearby talk amongst themselves
as I make my presentation.

Their private conversations cease.
My words take hold of their attention.
"Blah, blah, blah…" I continue,
then close.
My mouth cracks a thin smile
and my eyes sparkle with pride.
I have mastered the phone.

Those Who Follow

Go and drink the water.
Do not run to me if it tastes the same.
Follow as a lemming,
but don't cry when they forget your name.

Go and jump through the ring they hold.
Don't question when their word is told.
Follow them and drink behind that cloak,
but don't be thrown when alone, you choke.

Next Generation

I see a pudgy-armed child
reach for a book.
He studies it for a time
with a puzzled face.
Brought to boredom,
he places the book
back on the shelf.
It feels like a small, sad victory -
the boy simply paying it a thought.
But flashing lights
and the promise of violence
consume his attention.
The electronics of our age
pose a more immediate satisfaction.
He turns and walks away,
uneducated;
another uneducated child.

Love

愛

The Song

If life is a song,
then it is played joyously
from the organ of your heart.
For it had no lyrical worth
until you wrote it,
splashing the pages
with your colorful brilliance.
Nor did it have melody worth hearing
until you sang it in my ear,
whispering the tune
delicately above my lobe.
It resonates there,
echoing from heart to soul,
tying the two together
like beautiful twines of silk.
If life is a song then you sing it,
harmonizing the hours of the day.
I listen and consume that which is love.

The Coil Unwinds

You offered your promise,
then you left me behind.
Now I lie broken
and the coils unwind.

What is it that grabs you
and directs your mind?
What voices torment you
as the coils unwind?

You don a lovely smile,
but your tongue is so unkind.
You lure me like a siren
and the coils unwind.

I risk another scar
as our fates intertwine,
but you stun me with truth
before the coils unwind.

The past finally ignites,
then we leave it behind.
I see a subtle glimmer
and the coil, slowly it winds.

A Lonely Hue

Blind from doubt,
I live without.

Consumed by fate,
subdued with weight.

As silence confuses,
destiny misuses.

Inside, an aching heart bleeds
as starving disaster feeds.

Drowning its hunger with me,
swallowing all that would be.

Then light seeps through,
destroys the lonely hue;
erases the sad color -
a somber shade of blue.

Now absent of disbelief
I exhale waves of relief.

With blue driven into shadows
my soul is free from the gallows.

No longer in fear,
there's a single tear

in praise of what is new;
gone is the lonely hue.

Hourglass

I had a dream one restless night
that your love swirled 'round the moon
before offering itself at my feet.
It sliced through the crisp air
and showered the vapid ghosts with life anew
as it created whimsical circles of vibrant light.
Woe, I did not act in time to receive it;
the energy sputtered to a halt —

I was too late.

The same dream returned the next night.
What a horrible sleep it was.
I ran to grasp the light,
this time aware of its presence.
But again, I was too late.
Not wanting to trust the sanctity
of my inevitable future,
I delayed my embrace
and fell short in sopping earth —

I was too late.

It later came again,
for a third night of sorrow.
I opened my arms to welcome your beauty
and you tore through me like a bullet does the breeze.
I had delayed your trust too much to satisfy.

I was too late.

A likeness to that dream plays out
in the blinding light of day,
but on that account
I will not hesitate.

To Live Without Love

To live without love
is to live without peace.
The battles within
will erupt without cease.

A hollow existence
will forever endure,
benighted of the ardor
of fairytales and lore.

To live without love
is to wallow in scorn,
but to live without your love
is to linger forlorn.

All Along

Times change and feelings hide-away,
lying dormant somewhere beneath
the smiles and the frowns.

Times change and people lose hope.
The brilliant, beautiful dreams of love
become stamped out by nightmarish reality.

People wait and lose patience,
eventually moving on down the road
to something more immediate and solid.

Times change and people miss chances,
only to send them off to the next lucky
fool who stumbles in line.

Times change and people pass from this life,
embarking on their next great journey
with infinite possibilities.

And when it comes time for me to go,
to move on to my next adventure,
I want you to know
that I've loved you all along.

Through those wonderful eyes,
you see me in a way that no one else ever has.
Knowing that I have someone like you in my life
makes my life worth living.
Someone who, with one word,
can bring my day from depression to happiness.

Though I don't usually know how to show it
and I can't give you all the things
that you deserve,
I want you to look back someday
and remember that I've loved you,
all along.

And the Sun

The tide knows nothing
but to pull and break.
Just as time lingers on
for the seasons to take.

And the sun teases softly
a night that longs for grace -
a quick yet bottomless kiss
as it slips beneath God's lace.

I know the tide
will drift and die
and each season will pass
as shadows in our sky.

The sun will always touch
a yearning night in love,
only for a stolen breath
as it tumbles from above.

Such things will come to pass,
solemn moments of lust,
but the birth of sun each day
pulls my spirit out from dust.

The rising of the sun
spawns hope in me anew.
And this envious sun, like me,
will rise and fall in love with you.

I Am Blessed

I love you
with more rapture than the seas
as they wrap around the Earth.
For your shimmering hair,
shaming Rapunzel,
flows like the waves,
and I am touched.

I love you
deeper than the truth in those eyes
each time they lock with mine.
Angels fall from Heaven
to witness them glow.
We kneel before you
and we are blessed.

I need you
more desperately than a soul
who needs its mate to be alive.
You give the air unto my lungs
and the blood unto my heart
and I am saved.

I feel your passion
swelling inside of me
like an inferno dancing in silence,
bringing me to a place of utopia.
There, you whisper my name
and I am changed.

You reach out your hand
and I am loved.
Your flesh grazes mine
and I am moved.
You speak in the night
and I am freed.
You give to me your love
and I am blessed.

On This Day

On this day
when a mountain bends;
on this day
when poverty ends;
when waves deny the shore,
on this day
I will love you no more.

On this day
when trees melt beneath the sun;
on this day
when a pair is merely one;
when clouds refuse to ascend,
on this day
my love for you will end.

When rocks rise up from the ground
or a siren makes not a sound;
when feats of fiction prove true,
on this day,
I will no longer love you.

Blessed is the Rose

Blessed is the rose
that grows in your garden of grace.

Blissful is the one
who snatches a chance
of a trace
of a face
where beauty is growing -
in a place
where hearts beat for light.
Your garden
where laughter is flowing
and petals
are caressed into the night.

But broken is the rose
your hand touches upon the least.
And empty is the soul
who bleeds of a need of a feast
or a taste
or a glimpse,
all in haste
before it slips
into the waste
of what has been,
into the past
once again.

For dying is the rose
that has grown beyond your fingertips.
Yearning is the rose
who knows the warmth of your lips.

Blessed is the rose -
blessed, he who knows.

Eternal Felicity

To look at you
is to feel
the deep emptiness inside me
wash away.
Just like sand
on a jagged sea stone
as relentless waves
crash upon it.

To touch your hand
is to experience
the supernal feelings of forever -
Forever on my mind,
forever in my heart
and forever burned into my soul
is your love.

When I hold you close
and I feel our hearts
pounding as one,
I hold the heavenly body of an angel,
who in order to get her wings,
must take pity on a poor,
lonely wretch
and truly love him.

To have your benevolent eyes
fall upon me,
being without sin I am not,
is to feel cleansed
of all moral depravity
as if by God's divine light.

Your enticing voice,
which can only be claimed
by a near flawless human being,
is like a drug
that weakens my knees
and pierces my mind,
only allowing thoughts
pertaining to you.

Those words,
even combined with all the words
in any existing language,
still scarcely provide a prelude
to the nearly indescribable feelings
that I hold for you
deep down in the pit
of my eternal felicity.

More alone than I

Your heart is starving for something certain.
It shows in your eyes, it's there in your touch.
I can feed it, give it new life.

Your soul echoes a desperate call -
a cry for affection too long unheard.
I alone can hear it and answer.

The smile you wear is a false one.
The love that you present is not true.
This game of pretend has you suffocating,
but you can take the air that I breathe.
Without you, it is worthless to me.

At night, your tears fall to the floor.
There, they mix with your loneliness;
your neglect.
Combined, they create a somber mixture
and in it, you are stuck.
Cemented like a sad, beautiful statue.
But I can crack that rigid veneer.

For I am the one who sees your pain.
I am the one who hears your cries.
Allow me to dry your dampened cheeks.
Let me fill your life with something
other than disappointment.

Your heart knows it is the only way,
yet there you are with your companion
more alone than even I.

Night Shall Fall

Night shall fall
and day shall pass,
but this heart,
it will not waver.
I've made a choice
to hear your voice
and it is that
I wish to savor.

Crashing waves
will tease the shore -
salty castles
kept from drying.
Those tides will come
then leave again,
but my truth
will be undying.

My heart lost hope
not long ago
and decayed
within a tomb.
Then through a crack
hope came back-
Oh, how quickly
faith can bloom.

Stars will shine,
then go away
and leave a void
where once was light.
But birds will sing
and wind will bring
the melody
all through the night.

The sun will rise
and clouds will form
giving way
to peaceful rain.
And night shall fall

and day shall pass,
but my love
will still remain.

Ocean of Unwanted Love

I'm lost in the sea of my own questions;
plunged by the waves of unfulfilled promises.
Poseidon bestows no mercy on fools,
only quakes with laughter at their folly.
He and father time give lessons well taught,
but enforce their laws with brutal hands.
This cruelty renders me powerless,
helpless in an ocean of unwanted love.
I'm encompassed by an unreturned wanting
that tears the pulsating heart from my chest.
Crimson mixes with green
as my neglected vessel sinks ever further,
falling slowly to the cold depths where failure resides.
Finally, it reaches the ocean floor,
forever resting,
but never in peace.

Of Ambiguity

I don't have you.
I may never have you again
and it brings me to tears.
You will never see them though,
just as you have never really seen me.

I've never savored the harsh honesty
of being truly witnessed by you.
Instead, I was assaulted by restless glares
from your painfully beautiful face.

You've never glimpsed the heartbeat
behind your own reflection in my eyes.
Never seen the future in my dreams,
or the past in my failures.

I was a mere vessel;
a method to mask the beast
that laid in wait.

And mask it I did,
all too well.
So precisely, in fact,
that I began to share it with you,
come love or ruin.

Logic would suggest that
I am better off without you.
Perhaps, that is the truth.
Logic also says
that we will never be again.

But then,
love has never made much sense.

One Trillion Hearts

One trillion hearts
couldn't love you as much.
Together they would
delete their own honesty.
Their purpose would be
misread to themselves.
When compared, they would
be vague and unfeeling.

Their one trillion loveless vows
could not acquire the purity of my truth.
I would overwhelm their
meaning of devotion
and give it a new definition
of my own.

One trillion sleepless nights
is what I would face without you.
A lifeless dent in our bed
would be a constant reminder
of my heartache.
Thus spawning one trillion broken hearts -
one for each time I would see your face
in my dreams.

One trillion lustful journeys
could never replace the love
that binds between you and I.

One trillion beating hearts
could never love you as much
as mine does.

Passion's Kiss

You have witnessed my passion burn
high to the peaks that dreams can lend;
high where the air begins to end.

Where nimble cliffs
dodge my feet
and down I fall
and fail to meet
the dream that once
had made me whole
escapes me now
and take its toll

And to the grave
it wilts and falls
until the night
when darkness calls

Into my ear
so soft and clear
my passion speaks
it pulls me near

It shows me life
that has no end
as long as hope
is there to mend

It shows my life
perfection's bliss
and dreams reborn
from passion's kiss.

The Silence of a Life

I can feel the air around me -
it doesn't feel the same.
It hovers freely now about me,
but still it howls your name.
I love you deeper now than oceans,
with more expanse than the seas.
My need is greater now than absence
and the void of our deceit.
The leaves all fall in numbers,
but still they drift alone.
Like me, they wander slowly
into the vast unknown.
One by one they march in turn,
mere lemmings chasing death.
I too, now trudge along
always thirsty for a breath.
The black is thick here where I rest,
but still I see your face.
A heart sleeps here in my chest,
one that beats a tired pace.
Yet there is peace here in the black
amongst the silence of our choice
where I listen to perfection

..breathe..

where I listen to your voice.

Was There an Eye?

Was there an eye in the vacant land
where two hearts lived and died
that may have noticed my outstretched hand
left ignored as I cried?

Was there one about the garden
where once trod Adam and Eve
that took sight of a cherub's foot
with a twitch, preparing to leave?

Was there an ear to hear the sound
of the dying love coming 'round?
To listen to the noise
of pain as it destroys?

Was there an eye to catch the miracle
as you re-entered my heart and soul;
to witness the splendor of the day,
to see what remains untold?

Whom I Behold

As stars melt into the horizon,
tomorrow rests in their wake.
I behold a vision in my mind
as daylight is poised to break.

I dream of the distance apart
as light brings warmth to the cold.
Tomorrow is the ache of my heart
for you are the stars I behold.

A Perfect Morning

I know it to be a lie,
that the sun cannot shine
for the length of a day and night.
That the cool evening rain
cannot be as warm
as the late summer light.

And I know it to be true,
that beyond a luminous moon
hides a sky in shades of blue
and a sun that waits to swoon.

For I've seen the truth
of a perfect morning
and slept in the grass
still damp with crystal dew.

I've woke, I've loved
on a perfect morning
each time I woke
lying next to you.

As a Man

Stay with me, eternal,
and feel our passion grow.
Let me show you what I feel.
Let me tell you what I know.

You are still a brick
within my wall.
Indeed, if pulled
it all would fall.

You are still the thunder
in my cloud;
still the truth
behind the shroud;
still the whisper
that haunts my ear;
still the lyrics
I long to hear.

I love you as a bird
loves drifting through the sky.
I need you as a lake
needs a stream to stay alive.

I love you as a man
who needs you in his life.
I need you as man
who wants you as his wife.

Edge of Eden

It is to feel the way we feel right now -
the purpose of the promise of eternity.
The years will shed like skin
to the dusty floor of memory.
And with those years will fall the tears
and the laughter
and the anger,
the lust
and the love.

Though the moon will drift along
as time weighs heavy
on forever kissing souls,
the purpose of the promise of eternity
is to let the seasons flicker and fade
like a candle flame in the breeze.
But also, cherish those emotions
as if the first seconds of yesterday
were ticking away, only just.

To understand that
each glorious dawn
is a new reason to wake
and look into your eyes
and know those feelings remain.
To never question the words
my heart forms to speak to me,
but to learn the language as a second tongue
and speak it back to you
through our souls.

To be knocking on the door
at the edge of Eden -
at the foot of paradise
where so few spirits have even grasped
in their sweetest fantasies -
and know that we have found it
together.

All that is left to do is open the door
and step over the threshold

into our love's immortality.
That is the purpose of our eternity.
I promise you.

Garden

I walk in the garden
through flowers galore,
you look across
with eyes I adore.

I glimpse a playful smile
as you walk on cobble stone.
A snowflake slowly falls,
but then it melts all alone.

Oh, to be that cold wind
gently kissing your face,
or the jealous shadow
that tries to match your grace.

You look so perfect
in the retreating sun.
I can barely believe
I am truly the one.

The one with a kiss
blown in my direction
as another flake
melts on your cheek.

The one to receive
such tender affection
as you step over
an emerald creek.

All the flowers in the garden
bend as you glide on by.
Without eyes they still can see
a goddess from the sky.

As we finally join hands
I whisper over your way
to tell you that I love you,
and you look beautiful today.

How Fair, Indeed

How innocent is the grass
we step upon in the morn
as green leaps from the moisture
and the night retreats, forlorn?

How fair is the sprouting sun
seen parting the yonder hills
as light grows from its belly,
killing the fresh midnight chills?

How perfect could they hope to be,
despite this peaceful new dawn,
so close to your sheer glory,
fair and innocent as a fawn?

Envious do they watch and heed,
but how fair could they be, indeed?

Melodic Demise

I go through the motions
like a player on his pipe.
My fingers fumbling about,
but refusing to gripe.
I play the notes from within
and they howl through the air,
horrendous to be heard
impossible to bear.
Still she listens
as I grumble my melodic demise.
Tone deaf as always,
tears forming in my eyes.
She listens on
never wincing in pain
as I sing the love I know
party hushed by the rain.
Silence becomes my foe,
owed only my disdain.
Then I hear her crying softly,
partly hushed by the rain.

Once Upon a Midnight

Once upon a midnight
we wandered far and through,
walking in nature's forest
and drinking of twilight dew.

Once upon a midnight
we gazed with inquisitive eyes
on an image in the heavens
as our footprints marked the skies.

Once upon a midnight
your hand was given to mine.
I clenched it tightly to my chest
as we lost our sense of time.

Once upon a midnight,
we were free of daylight's mask.
we slumbered in the arms of love -
but was it a dream? I dare not ask.

Where You Will Find It

Upon lofty cliffs,
under pillars of salt,
beyond death's horizon
and damnation's exalt;

Over heights of no end,
despite eons of time,
within quantum strings,
and words that wont rhyme;

In dimensional planes,
through the black holes of space,
mid flickering flames
that fade with no trace;

Among outlines of shadows
that hide from themselves,
and long-cherished love notes
stacked upon shelves;

A mere taste of the spaces
from below and above;
a mere glimpse of the places
you will find it; my love.

Silent Echoes

You look up at the star filled night
wondering what you are searching for.
Your eyelids blink away a salty pool
as lightning breaks black once more.

A tear finds its way down your cheek
as light rain morphs into a waterfall -
deep pattering on your shield of armor,
forever drowning the sound of my call.

My silent echoes whisper through the breeze,
flirting ever so gently with your ear.
These echoes fill the canyons of your heart,
but never loud enough for you to hear.

Beautiful Rainbow

A beautiful rainbow
parting through the mist,
blessing the break of dawn,
wanting to be kissed.

A treasure waiting on the other side.
A chance to live where I once had died.
A palette of colors to fill my brush.
One last moment breaking the hush.

Holding On

How do you stop loving someone
when your heart beats slower without them?
How do you keep breathing
when there's no air left to force out?
How do you stop the moon from turning
when it's perched so far away from your grasp?
How do you quench a thirst
that is unending, deeper than the sea?
How can a man hold on so long
when he has no strength left to fight?
How do you stop loving someone
when they hold the biggest piece of your soul;
when you believe that they love you too?
How do you stop loving someone
when losing them was as close to death as you've been?
How can a man hold on
when the weight of it all feels like drowning?
How do you stop loving someone
when you know that it is real?
You don't.

No More Than Pain

Do not cry for me,
our tears are one and the same.
This feeling is nothing new,
it is no more than pain.

Do not be troubled by my scar,
it is but a blemish that won't go away.
It has become a part of my life
and it shows no more than pain.

Do not cry,
it's only a love we cannot show.
This is no more than pain,
this is all that we've known.

Do not cry for me that way,
for it will only be in vain.
Do not whisper to me that way,
it will bring me no more than pain.

Not the Rain

It is not the rain,
this curtain that falls
silencing your pain.
Cool and soothing,
melting disdain,
but no my dear,
it is not the rain.

It is not the sun,
though it feels as warm
as a winter flame.
It is not the sun,
but like that heat,
will never wane.

It is not the rain
out on display
since we fell in love
that perfect day.

Poetic

Your eyes are poetic
as they look all around.
Your smile is magnetic,
it lifts me from the ground.
This life is so hectic,
but the breeze brings a sound -
a voice so electric
my heart begins to pound.

Even absent from sight
the blind can all see
this angel from the light
bestowed upon me.
Poetic is the night
where your voice still runs free.
All the fates cannot fight -
this love is meant to be.

Through your hands I can feel
all the wonders above.
Alive and always real,
poetic is your love.

The Pebble and the Stream

I look for me inside you
the way I do within a dream.
I long to live beside you
the way the pebble does the stream.

I live to kneel before you
the way the sun presents a beam.
I live, breathe and adore you
the way the pebble does the stream.

Unspoken

Have I mentioned how beautiful you are,
how your face gives shame to a star?
You give jealousy to the proudest flower.
Have I mentioned that magnificent power?
The force that you hold over me
rivals the fearsome waves of the sea.
Did I forget to say those words
each time I held you close?
I should have said that above all,
you are what I need the most.

Whispers

Close your eyes
in waiting dark
and let the whispers
be your breath.

I want you

Feel the air
swell your lungs
and keep it
unto your death.

I need you

Part your lips
and taste the sounds
of the longings
that are left.

I love you

Forget your fears
and hold me close
and let my whispers
be your breath.

Forever

You Are My Violet

You are my violet
with flashes of brilliance
and you are my rose
that blossoms through stillness.

You are my daisy
with vivid love to share.
You are my violet,
beautiful and fare.

You are my lily
with petals the color of snow.
And you are my violet,
the loveliest flower I know.

A Feast of Words

Take these, my words
and chew them softly.
Swallow them down,
absorb them into yourself.
Such sustenance feeds
our ever blossoming bond.

And I live

Wings spread wide
and I live.
Seeing sin after sin
just to forgive.

Heart drumming steady
and I hear.
Tragedy impales again,
brings a salty tear.

Rise above the pain
and I feel.
Trust is offered,
never to steal.

Faith brought from despair,
finally able to give.
You offer me this hope
and that is why I live.

Dust

A gracious wind blows
and stirs the dying ground -
bitter, cracked, and dry
from a drought left unbound.

It swirls the parched remains
of a life with lonely hue,
so I'll grind myself into dust
and let the wind carry me to you.

Love Once Known

I catch you in the mist of mornings past.
I envision the power your speech has.
In your abode many days, but last
with you, my lover, or such as.

Inside my peace is pain that dwells.
Around my heart the stitching swells.
Without the heaven I once had flown,
I live without the love I had once known.

Space, Death and Love

Space is never ending,
it is timeless, free and wide.
It envelops all we know
like pedals 'round a bloom
with nectar deep inside,
while starving souls consume.

Death is ever reaching,
we must meet it all someday.
It comes with tears and light,
whether found or alone,
like clouds that fade away
or waves upon the stone.

My love is everlasting,
much like space and time and death.
From the moment of our meeting
and beyond my dimming flame,
with every desperate breath
my love will speak your name.

The Heart Grows Fonder

I know the stamina that love now takes,
from the sound your heart still makes.
When blended with the space between,
falling leaves in spring time are seen.

The bitter cold within my chest is felt.
If you were to touch my hand again
that frozen tundra would soon melt.

But how does a heart love over such space?
The answer is true in any parted case.
It is easy if you sit and ponder,
for absence makes the heart grow fonder.

All the Tomorrows

All the tomorrows that are to come
cannot replace the yesterdays
that have passed,
that were wasted,
that were spent with closed eyes;
the yesterdays that are gone,
that have left nothing
to take their place
but a dwindling bit of wax -
a dim flame flickering in the breeze
that comes with change
from day to day to day.

All the tomorrows may equal the sum
of all the yesterdays through to the last,
but only in countless hours.
They will not be wasted,
they will not be blindly spent,
they are not gone, for you still breathe
and in your breath there is the promise
of all the tomorrows that are to come.

Just as yesterday trailed slowly off
into the foggy mountains,
joining the spirits of dead love
and the memories of lost time,
tomorrow too, will drift away.
This poet, surely, will lose his rhyme.
But if your hope equals mine today,
tomorrow will not hold such a misty climb.

For all the tomorrows that are to come
will not shadow all the yesterdays
that we have known.
They will not delete the love
that passed between bodies
or blanket the truth
that passed between tongues
and eyes and ears and fingertips.
They will not be wasted
for your heart shames a pounding drum

and within your life is the promise
of all the tomorrows that are to come.

I will wait for tomorrow to come.

Blackberry Night Descends

Oh, blackberry night
how you deceive.
Blackberry night,
why must you leave?

We picked and searched
through fields of scent.
We loved and laughed
through night's descent.

A blackberry night,
it came and it went
as we followed the trails
that twisted and bent.

I held your hand close
as you tasted the taste
of the tart berry nectar
you consumed in such haste.

On your lips was a trace,
and in the air all around,
of the blackberry night
where a new love was found.

But blackberry night,
as all other things,
you must leave me alone
to fly with stained wings.

Life Brought Back

Troubling.
Thoughts recurring across time.

Confusion.
Eyes glazed with nothingness.

Unable.
Falling with a broken wing.

Destroyed.
Pieces thrown into a dark cave.

Numbness.
Mind searching for a key.

Hidden.
All doors cloaked by deceit.

Offered.
A chance to regain truth.

Taken.
A love so bright it darkens all.

Growth.
Trust overshadows dishonesty.

Complete.
Life forever wrapped in beauty's embrace.

The Heart of All Truth

So many mysteries to speak,
they consume all that I know.
Every thought a whisper
scarcely heard above the screams,
hardly voiced amongst the ruin.

So many questions rumble
like thunder throbbing the sky.
Questions that beg for truth -
a truth that is squandered by doubt,
dampened by a life without.

There are clues poised inside,
forbidden and cemented.
They will be freed not by my hands,
for you chip at their hardened cage.
And inside answers are breathing,
yearning to bounce at the sound -
the rhythm of your voice.

The shallow air becomes full and crisp
awaking honesty in a wasted pen
and the heart of all truth beats again.

A Blissful Treasure

It is a blissful treasure
which I seek -
to know your heart
and hear it speak.

Blissful tunes
will whisper past
and through my ears
unto the last.

The final word
that leaves your tongue
will bless my soul
and make it young.

And full of life
I shall be
for hearing you
whisper to me.

A blissful treasure
is all I ask -
to receive your light
and in it, bask.

And bask I will
with fortune's nod
and send my grace
unto our God.

With fortune's nod
your heart I'll seek
and in your ear
gently speak

of how I'd be blessed
and softly cry
to know your heart
until I die.

Cold Hands

Cold hands
touching my skin,
melting into my pours,
reaching farther in.

Warm caresses
filling the silent room,
fusing two lives together,
erasing empty gloom.

Warm caresses from cold hands
giving breath to a dying soul,
bringing me to dreamt of lands
and creating diamonds out of coal.

I feel more heat from you
than any bringer of flame.
Your cold hands spark my life.
My cold heart calls your name.

To the Stronger Goes the Love

I pass the light
in all its depth
from me to you
who is adept
to deal with love
in truest form;
to face the pain
and all forlorn.

My fumbling hands
with quaking nerves
can't hold my heart,
so now it's yours.
I pass the love,
the gift and gain,
with all I have -
my life, my soul, my pain.

Winter Again

I don't want to see the winter again.
It's too cold standing alone in the breeze.
I can't withstand the coming blizzard -
there is no shelter from leafless trees.

Our once resilient love,
a mere breath of what had been,
shall be a cold statue on the tundra -
a frozen relic in the glen.

The warmth of your kiss -
like sustenance.
I cannot bear the winter again.

Little Pieces

Little pieces of us,
grand like church glass,
though unstained.
Unblemished, untested
and unbroken.
Unbridled perfection.
Smooth clay ready for sculpting,
yet always holding true form within,
like a sculptor's premonition.
Statues of future lessons.
Foreshadowed greatness
waiting to be revealed.
Blessings of quaint size,
but infinite value.
Little blessings of life,
giving life greater meaning
than scriptures of the dead sea;
giving more truth
than the promise of cherubs,
and more voice
than a cavernous echo.
Little pieces of us,
like reflections
of who we are,
what we could have been,
and what we still could be.
We need only to live vicariously
through these little pieces
of us.

Enchantress

Enchanting spirit
grasping my tongue
with your beauty,
call my name.
Speak softly the words
that set me free.
Those words can be
any at all.

Enchanting spirit
at which I marvel,
never losing my gaze,
guide gently, my hand.
Lead my touch
to your gracious heart.
Let me greet your unstained soul
with my own, insatiable ache.

Enchanting spirit,
lilac amongst the night,
call my name sweetly
and give to me
your never wilting love
and give to me
my undying life.

When No One is Watching

When no one is watching
are you as lovely as you seem?
When every eye is closed
are you still perfection's dream?

Does your beauty exist
when light no longer holds sway?
When no one is watching
will your glory fade away?

Your lips steal my breath
each time they recite my name,
but when no one is there to see,
I will suffocate just the same.

In Defiance of the Sun

The sun came down
and said unto the earth,
"Let me sleep not
beyond your horizon
for I have seen beauty's apex
and it must be everlasting."
But the earth revolved, not obliging
the sun's request,
oblivious to the
rapture of perfection.

And the moon came down upon the earth
having heard of the sun's obsession.
"Where is this beauty that I must see?
It cannot be such that breaks the silence of the sun."
Though it was such beauty -
stunning and captivating like none the moon had seen.

But this vixen was not for touch nor taking.
She was a human and taken for life to a man.
So jealous were the celestial beings at the avarice of this man
that they waged such a war.
The sun and the moon wrought damnation on the man.
Still he fought for this woman.
Seven days and seven nights, the heavens screamed their jealousy,
but it was not enough.

The sun and moon knew nothing of love, only desire.
Such was the bond between this man and this woman
that even the heavens could not destroy.
Now, for eternity, the moon hovers in tribute to this love
and the sun rises in honor of this woman.

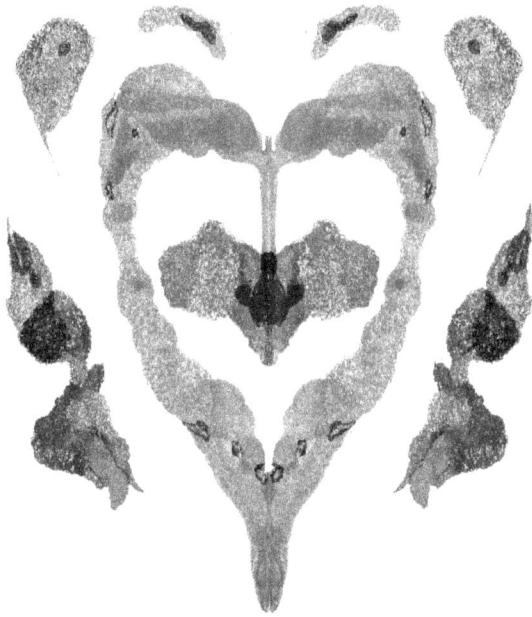

Scattered Ink by Kindred
Published by Savage Owl Press
Dallas, TX

www.savageowlpress.com
@kindred.author on instagram

permissions@savageowlpress.com

ISBN-13: 978-0692060582
ISBN-10: 0692060588

Cover by Kindred